HOW TO CHEER LIKE A CHAMP

CHEERLEADING SKILLS

WITHDRAWN

BY DIANE CECCHETTI

Enslow Elementary

an imprint of

Enslow Publishers, Inc.
40 Industrial Road
Box 398
Berkeley Heights, NJ 07922
USA

http://www.enslow.com

A special thank you to the cheerleaders and coaches at Inferno Cheer in Laconia, N.H., and Extreem Cheer in Hampstead, N.H., for their help with this book.

Enslow Elementary, an imprint of Enslow Publishers, Inc.

Enslow Elementary® is a registered trademark of Enslow Publishers, Inc.

Library of Congress Cataloging-in-Publication Data
Cecchetti, Diane.
  Cheerleading skills : how to cheer like a champ / Diane Cecchetti.
     p. cm. — (How to play like a pro)
  Summary: "Learn arm and leg movements, jumps, and voice control to cheer like your favorite squad"—Provided by publisher.
  Includes bibliographical references and index.
  ISBN-13: 978-0-7660-3208-8
  1. Cheerleading—Juvenile literature. I. Title.
  LB3635.C43 2009
  791.6'4—dc22

                    2007048518

Credits
Editorial Direction: Red Line Editorial, Inc.
Cover & interior design: Becky Daum
Editors: Bob Temple, Dave McMahon

Printed in the United States of America

10 9 8 7 6 5 4 3 2

To Our Readers: We have done our best to make sure all Internet Addresses in this book were active and appropriate when we went to press. However, the author and the publisher have no control over and assume no liability for the material available on those Internet sites or on other Web sites they may link to. Any comments or suggestions can be sent by e-mail to comments@enslow.com or to the address on the back cover.

♻ Enslow Publishers, Inc. is committed to printing our books on recycled paper. The paper in every book contains 10% to 30% post-consumer waste (PCW). The cover board on the outside of each book contains 100% PCW. Our goal is to do our part to help young people and the environment too!

Photo credits: AP Photo/Larry Steagall, 1, 19; AP Photo/Kevork Djansezian , 5; AP Photo/Connecticut Post, Christian Abraham, 6; AP Photo/Jane Mingay, 7; AP Photo/Donna McWilliam, 9; Deb Smith, 11, 12, 13, 14, 15, 16, 17, 21, 22, 23, 25, 32, 33, 35, 36, 37; AP Photo/Robert E. Klein, 20, 31, 44; AP Photo/Jose Luis Magana, 29; AP Photo/Eric Gay, 24-25; AP Photo/Pat Little, 27; AP Photo/Mark Humphrey, 28; AP Photo/Chris Pizzello, 30; AP Photo/Gerry Broome, 39; AP Photo/Ted S. Warren, 43; AP Photo/Darron Cummings, 45.

Cover Photo: AP Photo/Larry Steagall (large); AP Photo/Jim Weber (small)

CONTENTS

CHEER BASICS

Cheerleading began in the 1880s, thanks to a group of male college students. They became so excited during a football game, they stood in front of the crowd of fans to encourage them to cheer.

Women began to cheer in the 1920s. In the beginning, cheerleaders just cheered at games. In the 1970s, it began to change. Cheer teams started to have their own competitions. Today, cheerleading is a sport enjoyed by both men and women. It uses many physical skills such as gymnastics and dance.

Cheerleading Facts

- There are more than 3 million youth, high school, and college cheerleaders in the United States
- 83% of cheerleaders carry a B average or above in school
- 62% are involved in a second sport
- 83% are leaders in student organizations
- 81% of the nation's cheerleaders are between 14 and 18 years old

Many famous people have been cheerleaders. In fact, President George W. Bush cheered when he was in school at Phillips

Paula Abdul, pictured below with Magic Johnson, was a cheerleader long before she became a judge on American Idol. She cheered for the Los Angeles Lakers as a "Laker Girl" in the 1980s. She even had her cheerleading uniform retired by the team!

To learn more about the basics of cheerleading, see the resources listed on p.47!

Perfection

Cheer coaches have a saying: "Perfection before progression." This means that you should perfect each new thing you learn before trying something else new.

GETTING STARTED

With hard work, practice, and determination, you can become a great cheerleader. It takes physical strength, stamina, coordination, and flexibility. It is also very important to keep your body in great physical condition to keep up the energy needed to cheer.

A cheerleader is a leader, a friend, and an athlete. Just like other sports, cheerleading requires mastering specific individual skills. Each member of a squad needs to work at being a team player.

Cheerleading is a mix of dedication, strength, talent, friendship, and teamwork.

Teamwork

There's an old saying in sports: "There is no I in team." That's especially true in cheerleading. Working together is what makes a cheer team successful.

Hard Work Pays Off

This team from the Universal Cheerleaders Association saw its hard work pay off. They were able to travel all the way to England to cheer at a special New Year's Day celebration!

MOTIONS

When you watch an awesome cheerleading team in competition, what do you think makes it stand out? The difference between a "Wow!" performance and an average one is learning the correct basic motions and skills. Then add in some spirit, and you are a winner!

When cheerleaders lead the crowd they use hand motions, arm positions, and leg positions in different combinations to perform cheers during games or pep rallies. Basic motions and positions are very easy to learn, but they should not be overlooked. Cheerleaders who master these basics will have better cheers in the long run.

Learn the Names

The first step to becoming a great cheerleader is to learn the names of each motion and how to do them properly. Changing hand, arm, and leg positions is the starting point for creating new cheers.

Often there are specific hand, arm, and leg positions for each

Cheerleaders at college sporting events do lots of fancy stunts and gymnastics moves. Much of what they do uses very basic hand, arm, and leg positions and motions—the same ones they learned when they started!

HAND POSITIONS

The first things a cheerleader needs to learn are the basic hand positions. There are several basic hand positions that all cheerleaders use in their cheers. They include buckets or fists, candlestick, blade, jazz hands or spirit fingers, clap, and clasp. These hand positions are used routinely when performing cheers and chants.

When practicing or performing these hand positions, never bend your wrists. A bent wrist is called "broken wrist." Wrists should always be lined up with your arms. Your elbows should be locked if your arms are extended. When making a fist, the thumbs are tightly wrapped on the outside of the fingers. Fingers should form a "C" and the thumb should rest on top of the tucked fingers, not tucked under the fingers.

Finally, your shoulders should be relaxed, not raised like a shrug. In the clap and clasp, your hands should be under your chin, elbows in close to your waist, and fingers together for a clean, neat look.

Accuracy

It is important that arm positions are accurate and strong so that all team members look identical and one does not stand out.

Clap

Blade hands hitting together

Clap, Clasp

Clap or clasp is commonly used for cheers and chants.

Clasp

Thumbs and fingers wrapped around each other

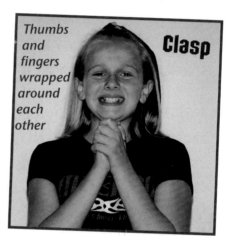

Make sure your hands don't come up over your chin!

Fists or Buckets

The majority of the time your hands are in this position. Pretend you are holding buckets in each hand.

Sharp & Snappy

Your arms should be stiff and your muscles tight, but it must look natural. You should punch your motions out with strength.

Extended, straight, separated fingers

Jazz Hands or Spirit Fingers

Blade

Extended fingers, straight and together

Arm positions add effect to the message of a cheer or chant. Your arm motions should happen in rhythm with the words in your cheer or chant or the music of your dance routines and stunts. It is important to use the proper arm positions to visually lead and excite your crowd. In order to be successful, every team member should be in sync. Moving together will catch the eye of your audience.

Coaches will often combine two or more positions to create a new cheer or chant. The punch is the most common movement used to create a response from the crowd. Other common positions are high V, low V, T, broken or half T, touchdown, low touchdown, bow and arrow, muscle man, dagger, box, punch, L, diagonal, K (right and left) and check mark.

Touchdown

Things to Avoid

• Over-extension of arms
• Poor arm levels
• Incorrect fist direction
• Bent wrists
• Circular motions or swinging of arms when going from one motion to the next

The "T"

Bow & Arrow

Broken T or Half T

Low V

Fists or Blades

Hand positions can be either fists or blades with most arm motions. Blades are commonly used with high V, low V, T, L, and touchdown positions, but can be in fists for variation.

High V

ARM MOTIONS

Once you have mastered all the arm positions, it's time to put them together into arm motions. How you move from one position to the next is just as important as doing the arm positions correctly.

Do not swing or make a circular motion when going from one motion to the next. Take the shortest distance to the next motion. Always make your motions sharp and strong. Finally, keep your motions in front of you. You should be able to see your arms and fists in the corners of your eyes while looking forward.

The best way to improve these motions is to practice in front of a mirror. It sounds easy, and it works. Watching yourself helps you see where you are hitting your motions and how you can improve them. So practice your motions at home. You can also try to get your team in a studio or gym where there is a huge mirror. You will notice your motions improving as you practice!

The "K"

Mirror, Mirror

When you practice in front of a mirror, watch as you hit your motions. Look for proper position of your hands and arms. Close your eyes and hit the motion. Then open your eyes and see how you did.

Diagonal

Punch

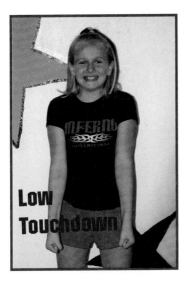

Low Touchdown

Combinations

There are many arm positions that go with the basic hand positions. The combinations are endless. Coaches come up with new ones all the time!

Building Strength

To develop strength in your motions you can do push ups to strengthen your arms and wrists.

Daggers

Check Mark

Beginning or Ready Position

Feet together, hands by your side, shoulders relaxed, hands in blades, and ready to begin

Cheer Position

Feet apart, hands by your side, shoulders relaxed, hands in blades, and ready to lead the crowd in cheers and chants

Lunge

One leg is straight with foot facing forward, the other leg is bent with foot facing out (be sure your knee is in line with your ankle). There are many variations to the lunge, such as right lunge, left lunge, forward lunge, and back lunge.

LEG POSITIONS

Leg positions are used together to change the look of a cheer, chant, or dance. Different leg positions can add levels to a dance or cheer. For example, a back row of a formation can stand upright while the front row kneels. The combinations of body positions create levels to give performances visual definition.

The most common leg position is the beginning stance, or ready position. Other cheer positions often used are the lunge, squat, and kneeling positions. Once you master these leg positions along with the hand and arm motions, you will have a good foundation. Then you can start to combine leg, arm, and hand positions to the beat of a cheer or dance.

Squat

Knees are bent out and lined up with the ankle, back is straight, shoulders are back.

Kneel

One knee is on the ground, the other knee is bent, and the foot is on the ground.

JUMPS

Jumps are more difficult to learn and master than most cheerleading skills. It takes a very long time to build up your body and skills to perform great jumps. This is where strength, energy, and flexibility are needed.

Stretching, conditioning and strength training provide the groundwork for awesome jumps. It takes a lot of hard work and individual commitment from the entire team.

To successfully perform a jump you must work on strengthening your hip flexors (the muscles around your hips), hamstrings (the muscles that run up the backs of your legs), abdominal muscles (belly muscles), knees, and ankles.

Exercises

To increase the strength in your legs so that you can jump higher:
• Run up and down stairs.
• Jump rope.
• Pick a spot on a wall. Jump and touch it 50 times with each hand, staying on the balls of your feet.

At a competition, judges look at the number and variety of jumps a team does, plus the timing and how well the jumps are performed.

Strength and Conditioning

Cheerleaders do strength and conditioning training to help with their jumps. Aerobic exercises (to strengthen muscles during long periods) and anaerobic exercises (to strengthen muscles in short, powerful stages) are both helpful.

These workouts help develop stamina and body control to do jumps, gymnastics, and to dance for longer periods. Strength exercises like push-ups, toe raises, straddle leg raises, tuck jumps, and V leg lifts will improve the way your jumps look.

TECHNIQUE

Just like any athletic activity, knowing the "right" way to do a cheer jump will help ensure that you do it well. It will also help make sure you don't injure yourself!

It is helpful to start your approach with an eight-count so team timing can be achieved. Keep your feet together, with your arms in a high V and your weight on the balls of the feet. Count "Five, six, seven, eight." Then swing your arms down past your sides and bend your knees as you count "one" and "two." On counts "three" and "four," your arms swing back up and you begin to lift. Rise up on count "five" and your legs leave the ground.

Jump into the desired jump position. Come down on count "six," and land lightly with your feet together and your knees slightly bent on count "seven." The final "eight" count is the clean-up for a polished ending. Arms come down to your side, your head is up, and your back is straight to avoid falling forward.

Jump Basics

There are four basic elements to a jump:
- Approach
- Lift
- Execution
- Landing

Getting the technique right makes for a clean look.

Approach

Lift

Landing

Abdominals

Lifting from your abdominals will give greater height. Pull up your head, chest, and shoulders and keep your back straight. Arms should be in a T position to begin.

When you are comfortable, the arms can be positioned to each specific jump. Toes should be pointed and arms stiff and controlled.

STRETCHING

It is important to stretch before you attempt to jump. Your muscles should be flexible to help you avoid injury. Make sure to warm up and stretch your legs, hips, and lower back muscles. If you do not stretch completely, you could injure a muscle. This could be a big problem during a busy cheerleading season, because the best cure for an injured muscle is rest.

Before You Stretch

Never start a workout by stretching. Start with light jogging to increase the blood flowing to your muscles. Then start your stretching.

Go Slow

When performing your stretches, warm up and progress gradually.

Lean slowly into each stretch.

Do not "bounce" in your stretches.

Increase the stretch gradually.

Be Careful!

Not everyone can do the "splits" or stretch as far as some can. Never over-stretch a muscle. You could injure it!

BASIC JUMPS

There are lots of jumps you can learn. But it is always best to start out with the basic ones and progress from there.

A cleaner jump will make you stand out! It will also get you a better score and put you up front in the routines. Here are some ways to clean up your jumps:

- Straighten your legs. Keep them straight from the beginning to the end (unless the jump requires your legs to be bent).

- Point your toes. It is an added touch that will distinguish a good jump from a bad one.

- Watch your motion. It needs to be sharp and you should not touch your legs, feet, or toes at any time.

- Watch your jump placement. Concentrate on your technique as much as possible.

- Keep your chest up. It will make your jumps look higher.

- Keep your head up. It will help you keep your chest up, and it shows you have confidence in your jump.

- Watch your wrists. They should be straight, not bent.

- Land with your feet together. It makes for a perfect finish.

- Squeeze and hold your landing to show everyone that you landed it perfectly.

Tuck

Knees facing forward and tucked up into the chest, toes are pointed downward

Toe Touch

Arms are in a T. Knees point to the sky.
Keep a straight back and "sit" into the jump.
Reach out toward your toes, but do not touch them.

Front Hurdler

One leg is straight, in front of the face. The other is bent, with the knee pointing down. Let your leg come to you. Don't go to it.

STUNTING

The risk of injury becomes greater when you begin to stunt. There are several rules that all cheerleaders must follow when it comes to stunting. The most important of these is that safety always comes first. Here are some basic safety rules:

- Always have an advisor, coach, or adult watching at all times. Never stunt until you are properly taught the techniques.

- If anyone feels uncomfortable or unsure about a stunt, do not do it.

- Always be serious about what you are doing.

- Spotters and bases, never take your eyes off the top person. They trust you. Never fool around— this is serious, and someone could get hurt!

- Top person, make sure that you have complete trust in your bases and spotters. Work to develop this trust relationship with all of your teammates.

- Everyone near a stunt should have their hands up and be ready to catch the top person the first time a stunt is done.

Make sure you are on a good surface, such as cheerleading mats. Never build a stunt on hard surfaces without a mat. Level grassy surfaces are okay, but check the area for rocks, glass, or holes.

Be Safe!

It's never safe to try a new stunt without an adult's help. Cheerleaders can suffer serious injuries if they try something too risky. A qualified coach can help keep you safe.

Hours of Practice

College cheerleaders spend hours and hours practicing their stunts and routines on mats before ever trying them on a gym floor.

STUNT GROUPS

A basic stunt group includes a base of at least two people, a top person, and a spotter. Bases are cheerleaders who hold up the top person. A base's main responsibility is to give solid support to the top person and to catch them during the dismount.

It is the top person's job to climb lightly and control her head, hips, arms, legs, and chest to balance the stunt. Careful timing and weight transfer help the bases and top person to build the stunt. The spotter's main responsibility is to protect the head, neck, and spine of the top person.

The spotter also provides extra stability and is often responsible for controlling the timing of the stunt by counting during building and the dismount. Bases and spotters are always on the ground.

Base Men

Male cheerleaders do a lot of work as bases. They lift, throw, and catch the lighter female cheerleaders.

But many male cheerleaders also do tumbling and other gymnastic moves, too.

Eyes look up

Keep hips, shoulders, knees, and ankles aligned.

Bases stay close together for better balance

Step, lock, and tighten legs.

Top Person (flyer)

• Know when, where, and how to place your feet, hands, and body into the base to keep balance.

• Keep your hips aligned over the bases. Flexing, stretching, and locking the legs will help maintain balance.

• Distribute your body weight and energy to help bases keep control and balance to complete the lift.

Spotter

• Control the building by helping the flyer climb.

• Stand close to the stunt, but not underneath.

• Maintain contact with the flyer for stability.

• Develop the ability to sense when a stunt will fall.

• Catch the flyer as high as possible.

• Protect the head, neck, and back of the flyer.

• Know the basic grips to catch the flyer.

Base

• Control your hips to keep the stunt group stable and balanced. This becomes difficult with the weight of the climbing top person.

• Sense when a stunt will fall and know what to do.

• Always release your grip on the feet of the top person for the dismount.

STUNTING

As you progress through the basics of cheerleading, you will begin to want to try things that are more advanced. Cheerleaders should never try a new stunt, dismount, or other skill without help from a qualified adult, however.

Cheerleading groups have a basic motto: S-P-O-T. It stands for "Save Person On Top." This means that during any stunt, the group should be focused on safety first, and performance second. And when focused on safety, the stunt team's primary concern should be the cheerleader who is on top of the stunt—the top person, or flyer.

The flyer is in the most danger because she is furthest from the ground. She also has the most difficult parts of the stunt to per-form. She is counting on her teammates to catch her at the end of the stunt. She is also counting on them to catch her if she falls.

All three jobs—base, spotter, and flyer—have important jobs in order for a stunt to stay safe.

Without strong, firm grips, stunting would be impossible. Working on good grips helps improve both the safety and the look of any stunt. Some grips are used during the building of the stunt only. Others are used during the stunt, and some are particularly helpful in dismounts. But all grips are key to successful—and safe—stunts.

Four-finger Grip

The base supports the upper arm of the top person with one hand, fingers facing forward and thumb in the back. The other hand is in the handshake position. This grip is used for suspended stunts and step-off dismounts.

Handshake

The bases join hands with the top person as if they are shaking hands. This grip is used for shoulder sits, chair mounts, and some basic dismounts for added safety.

Thigh Stand

The top person places her foot in the pocket with the bases in a lunge position. The inside arm of the base is wrapped around the top person's leg above the knee, with the hand either in a full fist or flat. The outside arms and hands of the bases grab the top person's foot.

Extension Prep

The bases hold the top person's foot in their hands at the heel and toe, holding at chest level. The spot holds the top person at the waist. As the stunt progresses upward to the shoulders of the bases, the spot holds the ankles.

DISMOUNTS

We have all seen amazing dismounts performed by college cheerleading teams. Twisting, spinning girls fly down into the waiting arms of fellow cheerleaders. They seem to do it without even thinking about it.

In truth, hours of practice have helped prepare the cheerleaders and built their confidence. And they all started with basic dismounts and drops from relatively low heights. No one should try a difficult dismount, such as a cradle, without first mastering basic dismounts.

The most basic dismount is the step off. In this dismount, the top person holds the outside hands of the bases while stepping forward, off the stunt.

The top person should bend her knees to absorb the landing. The spotter assists the dismount by holding the top person by the waist. The bases hold the top person's hands in a four-finger grip to control the landing. The bases and spotter take almost all of the flyer's weight for an easy landing.

Good Timing

The spotter helps control the timing of a dismount by calling, "One, two, three, down." This gets everyone started at the same time to help make sure the top person comes down straight and in control.

The spotter uses the arms to assist the top person for straight landing.

The top person holds her hands straight overhead in a clasp position. Arms must be straight so you do not hit the bases. Staying tight and keeping your back straight with the legs together will let you come down smoothly.

The bases push the top person's feet together with the help of the spotter. As the spotter counts "three," the bases shove slightly to let the top person drop straight downward. They assist by using their arms to catch her at the waist as she moves down.

CRADLE

The most difficult dismount is the cradle. Before attempting a cradle, make sure you have mastered the more basic dismounts. Also, make sure you are working with the supervision of a qualified adult.

The cradle begins with the bases doing a "sponge toss" of the top person. This is a short movement down with a slight push or pop up. This pushes the flyer into the air. The flyer kicks her legs forward and "sits" into the catch. The bases then catch her in their arms with the help of a spotter.

The bases and the spotter must be especially careful to catch the top person in a cushion-like manner to keep her from hitting their arms with too abrupt a force. They have to bend, or "give" a little with the catch, so the flyer lands softly. If they are not careful and prepared for the force of the flyer hitting them, it is more likely that the flyer will be dropped.

STUNTING

Good Catch

Each of the bases and the spotter play important roles in making a safe cradle dismount catch.

The bases catch the flyer on her back and under her legs. One catches the upper back and upper legs; one catches the lower back and behind the knees.

The spotter catches the flyer under her arms at a high point, to keep the flyer's head up.

The flyer keeps her legs together and her arms outstretched so she is easier to catch.

TUMBLING

Tumbling can be a great crowd pleaser. In the past, not as many cheerleaders did tumbling skills as they do today. Teams use tumbling to impress the audience.

The key to a skillful tumble segment is performing the skills as if the team was one. Practice and personal training strengthen the presentation. Tumbling is divided into two categories, standing and running. Both require lots of practice, technique, and strength training with a qualified professional.

As with other skills, technique, development, and safety are very important when learning tumbling. There is, however, basic tumbling that you can learn.

No one should ever attempt advanced individual tumbling instruction from a book. Your coach or gymnastics professional is responsible for teaching you the skills, but it is your responsibility to make sure your personal safety is the top priority.

Just like with other cheerleading skills, start out with basic, easy tumbling skills before progressing to more difficult ones.

Gymnastics

Gymnasts make great cheerleaders. Cheer coaches often encourage young cheerleaders to learn gymnastics in order to help them build strength, develop confidence, and learn great skills.

Standing tumbling skills seem pretty simple. They are often things that children do on their own all the time. But in order to perfect them for an audience or judges, they take a lot of practice.

As you work on these skills, be sure to practice them in a safe environment, under the supervision of an adult.

Forward Roll

Squat down and place your hands on the ground, shoulder width apart. Tuck your head in with your chin resting on your chest. Push with the legs and shift your body weight to the hands. Continue pushing with your legs and roll forward onto the upper shoulders. Keep your body rounded and your abdominal muscles tight.

Pushing with your hands helps propel you back to a standing position.

TUMBLING

Round-off

A round-off is an important skill to learn properly. It often comes before the advanced tumbling skills.

A round-off is a forward facing cartwheel. From the standing position, do a quarter turn. Begin the cartwheel and as you become upside down, your legs should come together in a handstand position. Follow by snapping down your legs to bring your body up to a vertical stand. Land facing in the opposite direction from when you began.

Cartwheel

Start with your feet together, then lunge forward with your favorite leg in front, the knee bent slightly, and your arms up by your ears. Reach sideways with your arm, kicking your leg up.

The other hand should follow with arms straight. Your other leg should follow. In an upside-down position you move into a straddle handstand position as the weight of your body shifts from the hands back to the feet. Legs should be straight in a V position.

VOICE CONTROL

In order to be an effective crowd leader, it is important to get the fans' attention. With all the noise during a game, it can be difficult to get the crowd's attention. How do cheerleaders do this?

There are four parts to voice control: articulation, expression, pitch, and volume. All of these elements are used when you cheer.

Articulation is speaking clearly so others can understand. If you want to engage your fans to join in the cheers, they must know what you are saying. Expression will accent the words in a cheer to draw attention and engage the crowd.

Your pitch, or tone, should be low but natural. High tones sound squeaky, strained, and irritating. Many times it is difficult to keep a low, natural tone because your voice will get high and squeaky when you are excited. It is important that you practice voice control.

Volume is one of the hardest elements of voice control. You must be loud enough to be heard, but not so loud that you drown out your teammates!

The first word in a chant or cheer catches the crowd's attention. The last word finishes the cheer with enthusiasm. For example, in "Go, Wildcats, Go," both "go" words are emphasized.

Voice and Motion

Using articulation can actually help you hit sharper motions, too. It is easy to hit motions on particular syllables when they are said in a clear, steady voice. For example, F-I-G-H-T can have motions hit on each letter.

Have Spirit!

Every cheerleader must have spirit. Your excitement in what you are doing will help the crowd (or the judges) be more excited, too! So have fun, and have spirit!

VOCAL TRAINING

Warm-up drills are used especially at the beginning of the cheerleading season to learn proper technique. This begins with breathing exercises. Breathing exercises, along with plenty of water, will enable you and your teammates to keep your voices healthy. You can protect your voice in a number of ways:

- Warm up and cool down your voice (just like you do with your muscles).

- Inhale deeply to get lots of air, and cheer while exhaling.

- Practice using a low-pitch natural voice.

- To relax your neck and facial muscles, fake a yawn; feel the muscles you use and stretch them.

- Use signs to help the crowd with the words to the cheers.

- Avoid cheering when your voice is hoarse.

Take a Break!

Do not overdo it when you are not feeling well. Do not cheer at all if you are sick. You are more likely to strain your vocal cords when you are not well.

BREATHING EXERCISE

1. Lie on your back on the floor with arms at both sides

2. Raise your tongue up toward the back of your throat and breathe in through your mouth. You should feel your lungs filling up.

3. Your belly should rise

4. Exhale with a "shh" sound

5. Repeat 5 times

WARM-UP EXERCISE

1. Keep lips closed and loosely together

2. Hum in a pitch that is slightly higher than your normal speaking voice

3. Count to eight while humming then count to eight and breathe

4. Repeat

When doing this exercise, try to make your forehead and nose vibrate.

GLOSSARY

★*base*—A person who holds and supports the weight of another person in a stunt.

★*cradle*—A dismount where the bases catch the top person in a face up, reclined position.

★*dismount*—A way to return the top person (flyer) to the floor after a stunt.

★*flyer*—The person that is elevated into the air by the bases; the person that is on top of a pyramid or stunt.

★*jump*—An action where both feet leave the ground; a coordinated placement of the arms and legs while the feet are off the ground.

★*motion*—A set position of a cheerleader's arms.

★*mount*—Any skill in which one or more people are supported by one or more people.

★*pyramid*—Multiple mounts or a group of stunts next to one another.

★*routine*—A presentation of cheerleading skills to an audience.

★*spotter*—A person located in back or front of a stunt to help control the stunt and for the additional safety of the flyer.

★*stunt*—Any skill or feat involving tumbling, mounting, a pyramid, or toss.

★*toss*—A throwing motion by bases that starts from the ground or waist level with the flyer becoming free from contact with the bases.

★*tumbling*—A gymnastic skill used in a cheer, dance, or for crowd appeal.

LEARN MORE

INTERNET ADDRESSES

★ **American Association of Cheerleading Coaches and Administrators**
http://www.aacca.org

★ **American Youth Football and Cheer**
http://www.americanyouthfootball.com/cheerleading.asp

★ **CheerWiz**
http://www.cheerwiz.com

★ **National Council for Spirit Safety and Education**
http://www.spiritsafety.com

★ **Pop Warner Little Scholars**
http://www.popwarner.com/cheer/

BOOKS

★ *Complete Cheerleading,* by Jus Carrier and Donna McKay. Champaign, IL: Human Ki   2006.

★ *Cheerleading: From Tryouts to Championships,* Editors of *Inside Cheerleading.* New York: Universe Publishing, 2007.

★ *The Ultimate Guide to Cheerleading,* by Leslie Wilson. New York: Three Rivers Press, 2003.

INDEX